ambridge and its Colleges

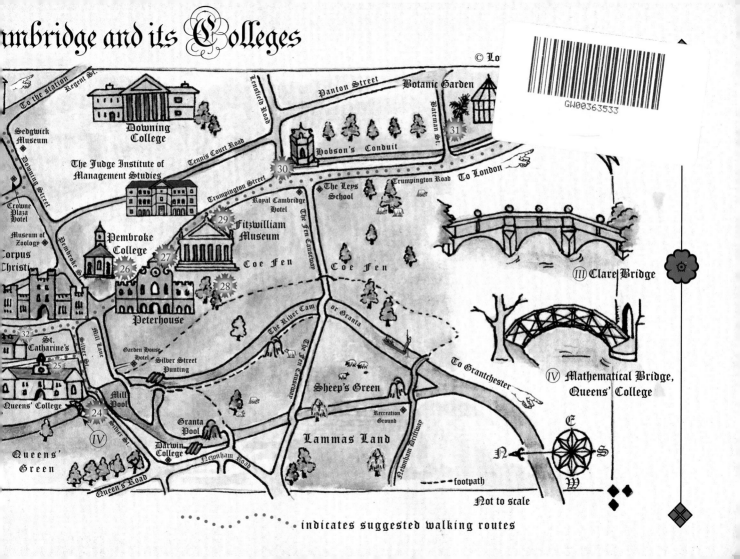

© Lo...

To the station

Regent St.

Sedgwick Museum

Downing Street

The Judge Institute of Management Studies

Downing College

Lensfield Road

Tennis Court Road

Panton Street

Botanic Garden

Bateman St.

31

Hobson's Conduit

Crowne Plaza Hotel

Pembroke St.

Museum of Zoology

Corpus Christi

Pembroke College

26

27

29

Fitzwilliam Museum

Royal Cambridge Hotel

Trumpington Street

The Leys School

Trumpington Road

To London

Coe Fen

Coe Fen

(III) Clare Bridge

28

Peterhouse

The Fen Causeway

The River Cam or Granta

32

St. Catharine's

Mill Lane

Silver Lane

25

Garden House Hotel

Silver Street Punting

Silver St.

The Fen Causeway

(IV) Mathematical Bridge, Queens' College

Sheep's Green

To Grantchester

Queens' College

24

Mill Pool

(IV)

Granta Pool

Darwin College

Newnham Road

Recreation Ground

Newnham Driftway

Lammas Land

Queens' Green

Queen's Road

E

N — S

W

footpath

Not to scale

indicates suggested walking routes

Photography © Andrew Pearce ARPS
Design & editing: Debi Pearce

First published 2009 © Fotogenix Publishing
Printed in England by Breckland Print
www.fotogenix.co.uk
ISBN 0-9547355-2-8

Also by Fotogenix Publishing:
'Cambridge: A Photographic Celebration'
'A Cambridge Keepsake'

Clare Bridge, 1638

The Cambridge Companion

Fotogenix
Publishing

*After the College Ball,
Senate House Passage*

Cambridge has been a place of importance since the Roman invasion. Small in size, big in reputation, it is renowned for its illustrious University, and the famous names, notable achievements and beautiful architecture that go with it. Signs of the past life of Cambridge are woven into the very fabric of the town. Street layouts have remained unchanged for centuries thanks to the permanent stone college buildings. Fascinating details of times gone by may be found in the stonework, paths, curious windows and quaint doorways. Ancient customs are preserved in the University's customs and displays of ceremony. Cambridge is proud of its past and nurtures its treasures.

The *Cambridge Companion* captures the essence of this lovely place. The illustrated map suggests routes that take in many delightful sights in the heart of town, (although some colleges may be closed at certain times). The red number icons by photographs throughout the book indicate their location on the map.

King's College, 1441

Cambridge University began in 1209, when scholars fleeing from riots in Oxford took refuge here. The first college to be founded was Peterhouse, in 1284, by Bishop Hugh de Balsham. Many early colleges were founded by the Church, others by monarchs wishing to create permanent places of learning. Colleges also came about following the ravages of the Black Death in Medieval times, when great numbers of clergy and learned men were wiped out and had to be replaced.

Today there are 31 Colleges, and around 15,000 students. Women were given their own colleges (Newnham and Girton) at the turn of the 20th century but it was not until the 1970s that the first female students were admitted to the other colleges. Degree ceremonies take place throughout the year in Senate House, with the majority happening in June. Immaculate ranks of 'graduands' process through the streets from their respective colleges, emerging from the ceremony into Senate House Passage as fully-fledged 'graduates'.

Above: Gate of Honour, Gonville & Caius
Left: Graduands entering Senate House

Timeline of Colleges

King's College Chapel, 1547

Clare College, 1326

Illustrious Cambridge Names

Charles Babbage, Henry Cavendish, Richard Baker	Peterhouse
Hugh Latimer, David Attenborough, John Rutter	Clare
Nicholas Ridley, William Pitt, Bill Oddie	Pembroke
William Harvey, John Venn, Alastair Campbell	Gonville & Caius
Admiral Howard, J.B. Priestley, Stephen Hawking	Trinity Hall
Christopher Marlowe, Matthew Parker	Corpus Christi
Samuel Pepys, Charles Kingsley, A.C. Benson	Magdalene
Francis Walsingham, John Maynard Keynes, Salman Rushdie	King's
Desiderius Erasmus, Isaac Milner, Stephen Fry	Queens'
John Addenbrooke, Ian McKellen, Jeremy Paxman	St. Catharine's
Thomas Cranmer, Alastair Cooke, Prince Edward	Jesus
Charles Darwin, Jan Smuts, Sacha Baron-Cohen (Ali G.)	Christ's College
Abdus Salam, William Wilberforce, Douglas Adams	St. John's
Isaac Newton, Rajiv Ghandi, Prince Charles	Trinity
John Harvard, Cecil Parkinson, Graeme Garden	Emmanuel
Oliver Cromwell, David Owen, Carol Vorderman	Sidney Sussex
John Cleese, Brian Redhead, Quentin Blake	Downing
Sylvia Plath, Germaine Greer, Emma Thompson	Newnham
John Selwyn Gummer, Hugh Laurie, Clive Anderson	Selwyn

Clare College Entrance

The Wren Library, 1695

Trinity College 1546

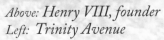

Above: Henry VIII, founder
Left: Trinity Avenue

Punts at Trinity College

Trinity Lane

St. John's College, 1511

The Bridge of Sighs, 1831

New Court, 1831

Great Gate, Trinity College

14

The Round Church, 1130

Magdalene College
1428

Some Cambridge Nobel Prize Winners

Jesus College, 1496

Nobel Prizes were first awarded in 1901. Since then, 83 have been awarded to members of Cambridge University: more than any other institution, with 32 won by Trinity College. Listed here are some of those great achievements.

Year	Name	Field	Achievement
1904	Lord Rayleigh, Trinity	Physics	Discovered Argon
1906	J.J. Thomson, Trinity	Physics	Electrical conductivity of gases
1925	Austen Chamberlain, Trinity	Peace	Work on the Locarno Pact
1927	Charles Wilson, Sidney Sussex	Physics	Invented the cloud chamber
1933	Paul Dirac, St. John's	Physics	Work on quantum mechanics
1935	James Chadwick, Caius	Physics	Discovered the neutron
1945	Ernst Chain, Fitzwilliam	Medicine	Discovered Penicillin
1947	Edward Appleton, St. John's	Physics	Discovered the Appleton Layer
1950	Bertrand Russell, Trinity	Literature	A History of Western Philosophy
1958	Frederick Sanger, St. John's	Chemistry	Structure of the Insulin molecule
1959	Philip Noel-Baker, King's	Peace	Work towards global disarmament
1962	Francis Crick, Caius/Churchill James Watson, Clare Maurice Wilkins, St. John's	Medicine	Determined the structure of DNA
1964	Dorothy Hodgkin, Newnham/Girton	Chemistry	Structure of compounds used to fight anaemia
1972	John Hicks, Caius	Economics	Equilibrium theory
1979	Alan Cormack, St. John's	Medicine	Developed CAT scans
1984	Richard Stone, Caius	Economics	Developed national accounting system
2000	Paul Greengard	Medicine	Discoveries concerning signal transduction in the nervous system
2008	Roger Y. Tsien, Caius	Chemistry	Discovery & development of green fluorescent protein GFP

Sidney Sussex College, 1596

Bridges of the River Cam

Cambridge Market Square

It was the Romans who established Cambridge as an important trading centre. Cambridge was once accessible from the sea, and business boomed through the Danish occupation and the dark days of the Normans. King John granted it freedom of trade in the 1200s, and the advent of the railway in 1845 further enhanced the town's prosperity. In Cambridge's days as a port, the little canals leading from the river along the Backs accessed trading stalls. As the river silted up during the 1600s, flat-bottomed barges were used, and in the early 1900s it was often possible to walk from barge to barge all the way between Queens' Mathematical Bridge and the Mill Pool.

A market has existed for over 1000 years, but not always as it is seen today. The Great Fire of Cambridge in 1849 destroyed a central cluster of houses in the market square. Until this date the fountain head of Hobson's Conduit had stood here since 1574, but was moved to its present location when the area was rebuilt. The market continues to thrive.

Great St. Mary's 1478

Christ's College, 1505

The Master's Lodge

Emmanuel's
Wren Chapel, 1677

Emmanuel College, 1584

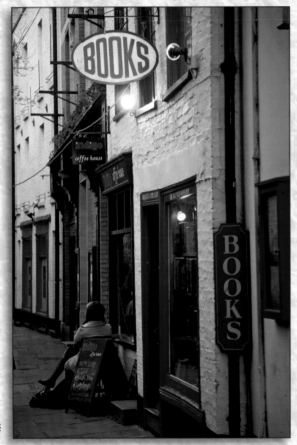

23

St. Edward's Passage

22

The Corn Exchange

In the heart of Cambridge

Ryder & Amies, by King's College

Queens' Mathematical Bridge, 1749

25

24

Queens' College, 1448

Pembroke College, 1347

Trumpington Street

Peterhouse, 1284

Peterhouse Deerpark

The Fitzwilliam
Museum
1816

Hobson's Conduit, 1574

The Botanic Garden, 1846

St. Catharine's College, 1473

Some Famous Cambridge Writers

1608–1674 John Milton, Christ's — Paradise Lost, Paradise Regained

1716–1771 Thomas Gray, Pembroke — Elegy Written in a Country Churchyard

1770–1850 William Wordsworth, St. John's — I Wandered Lonely as a Cloud, By the Sea

1772–1834 Samuel Taylor Coleridge, Jesus — Kubla Khan, The Rime of the Ancient Mariner

1788–1824 George Byron, Trinity — She Walks in Beauty, Don Juan

1809–1892 Alfred Tennyson, Trinity — The Charge of the Light Brigade, The Lady of Shallot

1882–1956 A.A. Milne, Trinity — Winnie the Pooh, The House at Pooh Corner

1879–1970 E.M. Forster, King's — A Room with a View, Howard's End

1882–1941 Virginia Woolf, Newnham — Mrs. Dalloway, To the Lighthouse

1887–1915 Rupert Brooke, King's — The Soldier, The Old Vicarage, Grantchester

1894–1984 J.B. Priestley, Trinity Hall — Angel Pavement, Lost Empires

1898–1963 C.S. Lewis, Magdalene — The Chronicles of Narnia, The Space Trilogy

1930–1998 Ted Hughes, Pembroke — The Iron Man, Hawk Roosting

1932–1963 Sylvia Plath, Newnham — Lady Lazarus, Tulips

Corpus Christi Clock 2008

King's College Great Gate, 1822

34

King's College Chapel, 1547

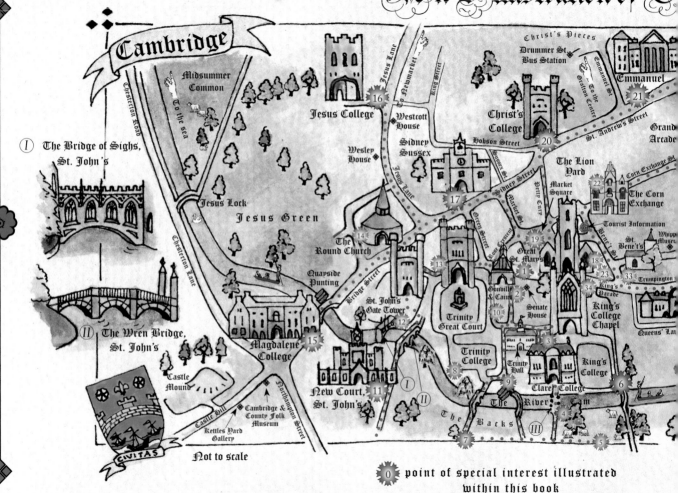

Cambridge

Jesus Lane
To Newmarket
King Street

Christ's Pieces
Drummer St
Bus Station

Emmanuel St
To the
Grafton Centre

Emmanuel

21

Midsummer Common

To the sea

Jesus College

Westcott House

Wesley House

Christ's College

St. Andrew's Street

Grand Arcade

I   The Bridge of Sighs, St. John's

Jesus Lock

Jesus Green

Sidney Sussex

Hobson Street

Sidney Street

The Lion Yard

Market Square

Corn Exchange St

22

The Corn Exchange

17

Tourist Information

St. Bene't's

Whipple Museum

Chesterton Road

Chesterton Lane

The Round Church

14

Quayside Punting

Green Street

Rose Crescent

Petty Cury

Market Street

19

Great St. Mary's

Trinity St.

18

23

33

Trumpington

II   The Wren Bridge, St. John's

Bridge Street

St. John's Gate Tower

13

12

Trinity Great Court

Gonville & Caius

2

10

Senate House

King's Parade

34

King's

King's College Chapel

Castle Mound

Magdalene College

Northampton Street

New Court, St. John's

15

11

I

8

Trinity College

Trinity Hall

3

Clare College

King's College

6

Castle Hill

Cambridge & County Folk Museum

Kettles Yard Gallery

II

9

The River Cam

4

Queens' Lane

CIVITAS

Not to scale

The Backs

7

III

5

0   point of special interest illustrated within this book